BCS
Improving Productivity Using IT

Level 2

Published by

CiA Training Limited

Release BCS012v1

D1335471

Published by:

    CiA Training Ltd
    Business & Innovation Centre
    Sunderland Enterprise Park
    Sunderland SR5 2TH
    United Kingdom

    Tel: +44 (0) 191 549 5002
    Fax: +44 (0) 191 549 9005

    E-mail: info@ciatraining.co.uk
    Web: www.ciatraining.co.uk

    ISBN-13: 978 1 86005 826 4

Aims

To provide the knowledge and techniques necessary to plan, evaluate and improve procedures involving the use of IT tools and systems which will improve the productivity of work activities.

Objectives

After completing the guide the user will be able to:

- Select IT tools and techniques to complete a given task

- Understand what expectations and requirements must be met by the task solution

- Understand what is required by a task and the best way to achieve it

- Evaluate the outcome of the task including strengths and weaknesses

- Identify improvements relevant to future work

      © *CiA Training Ltd 2009*

Contents

Section 1
Plan and Select

By the end of this Section you should be able to:

Describe the Purpose for using IT

Describe what methods, skills and resources will be needed

Plan how to carry out tasks using IT

Describe any factors that may affect the task

Select IT systems and software applications

Explain why particular IT applications were chosen

Describe any legal or local guidelines or constraints

Exercise 1 - Purpose

Guidelines

The solution to any problem starts with the problem itself. The first step in developing an IT solution must be the correct identification of what exactly is required.

Questions to be asked are:

- What is the purpose of the IT task?

- Who will be using it?

- What information will be required?

- How and where will it be used, for example, on screen or as a printed document?

- When is the solution required?

In a practical situation these questions will require you to communicate with the people involved. Hold meetings with the staff involved, both collectively and individually. Gather information on the problems facing them and investigate their requirements for a solution. Make sure you know what the problem actually is; people may be talking about the symptoms of the problem rather than its cause.

The intended audience can have a major impact on both the content and style of the final document, e.g. a report on company performance may be different if intended for the general staff or for the Financial Director, and a letter to a friend would look different to a business letter to a customer.

With technical content you should also be aware of the level of knowledge the audience has of the subject and plan the document accordingly. Too much explanation of areas with which the audience is familiar may cause them to lose interest. Likewise, too little explanation for an audience with little or no subject knowledge may have the same effect.

Consider too the cultural background of the audience and make sure that both the content and style are relevant and appropriate.

In the assessment for this unit, you will be given a scenario in which the purpose of the task is well defined. You should read the details of the scenario carefully and make sure you can answer all the questions listed above.

Having specific and documented aims is useful as it helps keep the development 'on course'. Constantly checking against the original project aims can prevent effort being spent on areas that are not relevant.

Exercise 1 - Continued

Examples

Three sample scenarios will be used throughout this guide to illustrate the points of each exercise. Each one will represent one of the original software applications, word processing, spreadsheets and presentations, which could be used in the assessment.

1. You are asked to produce a newsletter for the members of staff in your organisation. A selection of information items will be provided for inclusion, but not all of them will be used. The newsletter will be in printed form and needs to fit on two sides of an A4 sheet. You have been told that it must look professional, eye catching and appeal to all members of staff.

    The newsletter is to be produced on a monthly basis, with a consistent appearance. Not surprisingly, given the nature of the assessment, you have only one hour to complete the task.

2. You are asked to produce a brief introduction to your organisation to be viewed by all new starters as part of their induction process. This will be available as a continuously running show on the company intranet. It should consist of six screens of summarised information (a selection of possible information will be provided) with a consistent professional look and incorporate some degree of animation. It should be ready for viewing by the first starters in one hour.

3. You are asked to produce a system to work out the gross pay (before tax) for hourly paid staff in your organisation. Details of the hourly paid staff will be supplied, including their basic hourly rate. The system must allow the entry of the number of hours worked and any relevant bonuses for each person. The correct gross pay will be worked out for each person, including additional payment for hours worked above the basic number. Accuracy is obviously of prime importance.

    A report of the final figures is required each week by the factory manager. The system will be operated by the finance department staff who have a basic knowledge of IT office systems.

Note: It should be stressed that these are CiA sample scenarios, meant only to illustrate some of the features of the assessment. They have no connection with any scenario which may form part of the testing of this unit.

Exercise 2 - Application Choice

Guidelines

With the purposes of the task established, it is now time to consider possible IT solutions. In a practical situation it is worth investigating whether an IT solution is appropriate at all, or whether a combination of applications may be required. In this assessment it is assumed that a single software application is appropriate.

You will have to decide and justify which software application is best suited to the task you have been given. The following notes will help to understand the differences between the common software applications and appreciate their separate uses.

Word processing

One of the most widely used applications on computers is word processing. Word processing software such as *Microsoft Word* enables you to produce professional looking, well-styled documents for many different purposes. Typical word processing solutions include:

- Letters

- Mail shots

- Brochures/newsletters

- Reports

Word processing is appropriate for any task that requires a largely text based solution, particularly if printed output is required. Entry, presentation and formatting of text are easily handled by an application such as *Microsoft Word*. It is also easy to include different types of objects such as images, tables and charts. Many more specialised features are available, such as automatic creation of referencing like contents and index pages, and the ability to merge documents with data in tabular form to produce mail shots, etc.

One advantage of word processing applications for solutions that will be used by other people is their widespread use and acceptance. More people will be familiar with word processing than probably any other application.

Presentation

A presentation is an appropriate application for any task that requires a more visual result with text restricted to brief notes or bullet points, particularly if on-screen viewing is required.

Exercise 2 - Continued

Microsoft PowerPoint allows complex and impressive presentations to be produced with relative ease. The presentations can be used as on-screen shows controlled by a presenter, overhead projector shows, or for creating automatically run presentations for use as promotions in public places, or display on a network such as the Internet. They can include text in any format, pictures, organisation charts, graphs, sound and film clips, and information from the Internet. A slide show can incorporate impressive text animation and slide effects.

As well as slides, *PowerPoint* can produce presentation notes, handouts, printouts of slides and outlines of text. Presentations are excellent tools for promotional or staff training purposes.

Spreadsheet

Spreadsheets are most commonly used to manipulate figures. They can be used in:

- Accounting

- Cash flows

- Budgets, forecasts, etc.

- Transaction analysis

Any task involving the use of numbers can be done using a spreadsheet.

A spreadsheet package such as *Microsoft Excel* is a computer program created specifically to help in the processing of tabular information, usually numbers. The spreadsheet stores information in rows (across the screen) and columns (down the screen), forming a worksheet (the *Excel* term for a spreadsheet).

The biggest advantage that a spreadsheet has over other methods of manipulating data - using a table in a word processing application for example, is its ability to constantly update figures without you having to do any calculations. Once a spreadsheet is set up correctly, with formulas and functions, its calculations will always be accurate and any changes in data are recalculated automatically.

Spreadsheets can also take basic data and present it in an attractive way, for example as formatted lists, tables or graphs. More complex features are available such as conditional formatting, data validation, complex formulas, linked data, hyperlinks and a range of chart types. One particular advantage in using a spreadsheet application is its ability to handle complex analysis tasks, using such features as pivot tables, data tables, scenarios, sorting/filtering and sub-totalling.

         © *CiA Training Ltd 2009*

Exercise 2 - Continued

Examples

1. The newsletter scenario (see Exercise 1) requires a word processing solution. This is because the solution involves extensive use of text and needs to be printed out as a single double sided sheet. If the solution required the newsletter to be viewed on screen, on an intranet for example, then a solution using a presentation or web site application could be considered, but given the concentration on text, word processing should be the selected method.

    The solution could also have been created using an application such as *Microsoft Publisher*, but at this level, word processing would probably be chosen because of greater familiarity.

2. The induction program scenario requires a presentation solution. This is because the scenario requests summarised points on screen with animation, running as a continuous show. A presentation application such as *PowerPoint* is the ideal way to achieve this.

3. The payroll scenario requires a spreadsheet solution. This is indicated because the solution will mainly involve the repetitive processing of numeric information. The solution could also have been created using a database application such as *Microsoft Access*, but at this level, a spreadsheet would be the simplest alternative.

Exercise 3 - Justification

Guidelines

Having decided on an IT application which meets the needs of the current task, you should be prepared to justify your choice of application. This includes justifying the use of an IT solution rather than a manual approach. Although for the purposes of this qualification it is assumed that an IT solution will be implemented, you should be aware that in the real world the overall use of IT within an organisation would have to be considered before coming to any conclusions about solutions.

Within an organisation, there may be a variety of issues which affect people's attitude to IT.

- People who have never had exposure to IT systems can be wary of it because of unfamiliarity.

- People may distrust IT because they see it as intrusive and capable of monitoring their activity.

- People may favour IT solutions because they like the flexibility and the possibility of home working, for example.

- Some see IT systems as environmentally friendly because they can reduce the use of paper, for example, others could consider them environmentally unfriendly because of their reliance on electrical energy.

There are many benefits which can result in general from using an IT solution:

- For any given task it will usually be quicker to use an IT solution. In general an IT system will produce results, e.g. calculations, documents, more quickly than a manual process. This is particularly true for repeated tasks, as there is always the 'overhead time' of producing the original solution which will not apply when the task is repeated.

- An IT solution should be more convenient to produce as all the necessary information and functions will be available from a single point, the computer.

- An IT solution should produce more consistently high quality results, without the time and expense of employing specialists.

- An IT solution should produce more consistently accurate results. This of course depends on the input data being accurate.

- An IT solution should have a productivity benefit, as staff will spend less time performing and checking manual tasks.

Exercise 3 - Continued

- An IT solution should have a cost benefit to the organisation (as a result of all the points listed above being true).

- An IT solution should help to produce more integrated and consistent (streamlined) processes throughout an organisation. This can result from using the same fonts, colour schemes, imagery, etc., across a range of processes and by integration of data across processes. For example the results of a spreadsheet process can be easily used in the creation of a report.

It should also be noted that there are potential negative aspects to IT solutions:

- An IT solution has a development time and cost. This should be weighed up against the time and cost benefits.

- Be aware that people who will be asked to run any new IT system must have the necessary skills to do the tasks efficiently. This may involve retraining.

Examples

1. Word processing is the ideal solution for the newsletter task. It is a quick and simple way to produce a good looking document. The only alternative would be to use specialist printers and publishers which would involve much more time and money. Non IT staff could easily take over the production of future editions if a template were produced.

2. Similarly, an application such as *PowerPoint* is the only practical way that a professional looking presentation could be produced easily and quickly. Alternatives would be to employ specialist film makers.

3. The purpose of the wages task is to calculate and print a list of total pay for hourly paid staff. Using a spreadsheet application to do this will create an efficient solution with the minimum of manual processes. Once the rate details are entered and checked, the only weekly input will be a list of hours and bonuses for each person and the result will be a list of consistently accurate gross pay figures.

Exercise 4 - Planning

Guidelines

When the purpose of the task has been fixed, the details of the project need to be planned.

When planning your chosen task, some thought should be given to how you are going to obtain the desired result. The planning should include the content and explain where that content fits into the finished resource. Think about who the resource is for, how they would like the information to be presented and how it is to be used.

At this level your planning should pay particular attention to these points:

- The application to be used. This was covered in Exercise 2.

- Source material. What source information will be required and where will it come from? If it is an external source, some evaluation and validation may be necessary.

- Content. Are there any special requirements for the format and structure of the system output? There may be a house style which must be adopted, or the use of specified images and logos.

- Priorities. If there is more source material than needed for content, what or who will decide the priorities for which information will be used? If there are time constraints, which features must be included and which could be left out?

- Resources. What resources will be necessary to run the solution? For example, is any extra hardware or software needed, and will any extra personnel be required? Resources can include such things as:

  o Hardware - how many personal computers are available and what specification are they?

  o Software - what software applications are available?

  o People - how many people are available to operate any new system and will any more be required?

  o The skills and capabilities of the potential users. Do not attempt a project that will be technically beyond their abilities to operate. Be aware of what skills will be required, and consider a training process if necessary.

Exercise 4 - Continued

○ Your skills and capabilities. Do not attempt a project that will be technically beyond your ability to develop successfully.

○ Support - what level and amount of support will be available?

○ The needs of the organisation. You should not be developing projects for the sake of it. There should be clear definable objectives from the point of view of the organisation which justify the project. These objectives can be reviewed on completion to see how well they have been met.

Examples

1. In the newsletter scenario, all content would be provided, but there may be more than is required to fill two A4 sheets. Select the most appropriate data based on the task specification. A newsletter should contain news, so include items that are most current and have most impact on the organisation. However part of the specification was that it should appeal to all members of staff, so human interest stories could be more appropriate than accounting analysis reports. A newsletter would normally contain brief, summarised content rather than lots of detailed text.

    Any style and layout considerations will be provided, but as the newsletter is to be 'eye catching', try to include a range of formatting features such as different fonts, font sizes and colours. Include images if possible.

2. In the induction presentation scenario, all content would be provided, but again there may be more than is required to fill the six screens specified. Select the most appropriate data based on the task specification. Include content that will be relevant to new starters. This may include basic information about the company, some kind of organisational diagram, summary of terms of employment and benefits review.

    Use any styles and logos that are specified. As animation is specifically mentioned, plan to include some simple effects such as slide transitions. Keep the original specification in mind and remember, for example, that the presentation must be free running (looping).

3. The wages spreadsheet would probably have less emphasis on style and layout, although of course it should be clear and easy to understand. The main requirements are the system will be that it is accurate and easy to operate. All starting data would be provided, but check to see if it is all required. For example, it would not be advisable to include address details for the employees in such a system even if they were provided.

Exercise 5 - Factors

Guidelines

In completing any task there are a great number of factors to be taken into account to ensure a successful solution. Many of them have been covered in previous exercises but they can be summarised here with some additional points.

- Resources - are all of the required resources going to be available?

- Information – is all of the information required by the task going to be available?

- Timescale - are there limits as to when the solution must be available?

- Costs - are there limits as to the development costs of the solution?

- Style and format - are there any particular requirements for style (eye-catching, simple, amusing, etc.) which may affect the form of the solution?

- External factors - what impact will the solution have on people outside the organisation, e.g. Customers, Suppliers, Public?

- Personal preference - are there any strongly held personal preferences which may affect the form of the solution? The importance of this factor depends largely on the importance of the person with the preferences.

- Advance steps – are there any steps, maybe arising from the points above, which will require completing in advance of the task? For example ordering new hardware/software, or evaluating data sources.

Examples

1. For any scenario used in this assessment, the factors that may affect the task will be included in the scenario specification. For example, restrictions on time, cost or appearance. When planning the solution, take all such factors into account.

Exercise 6 - Local Constraints

Guidelines

As well as the requirements and constraints of the individual task which have been discussed previously, there may be more general constraints. Some of these may be in the form of local constraints such as existing 'house styles' in force within the organisation, and security considerations.

- House styles. In your chosen task you may already be required to format all work to specified house styles. These are formatting parameters that are set by an organisation to be applied to all documents used. They will include features such as which text fonts and sizes should be used in any given part of a document and which colour schemes and logos should be included. There may be variations of house style for different applications, e.g. for internal and external documents and for particular projects or product brands within the organisation.

- Security. Any solution should take into account data security. Data security can be broadly divided into two areas: security against data loss and security against unauthorised access. The effects of data loss can be minimised by ensuring that your solution is backed up, i.e. copied to an alternative location, preferably off-site, and that it is included in any existing regular backup procedures.

  Protection against unauthorised access will depend on how sensitive the information is in your solution. **Information security** is a term used to describe methods for ensuring that data stored on a computer system is protected against being compromised, or against unauthorised access. It can include such features as:

  o   A user ID/password policy to cover access to all computers

  o   Separate user level security on individual systems/data files

  o   Designated personnel responsible for each level of security

  o   Anti-virus measures, including use of a firewall

  o   Procedures for educating staff about their responsibilities regarding information security

  o   Security is particularly important when the data contains personal data about individuals. Storage and use of such data is governed by strict legal regulations, contravention of which can lead to criminal proceedings. All users of such systems must be aware of the relevant legislation, i.e. the Data Protection Act. This is covered in the next exercise.

Exercise 6 - Continued

Examples

1. A newsletter task will almost certainly involve the use of 'house styles' to ensure that the publication is representative of the organisation's image. Any style requirements will be given with the original specification.

    Although all required images and text will be supplied, in a real situation they should all be checked for copyright issues.

    There is probably no requirement for security on such a system, although the content could be password protected to avoid mischievous alterations.

2. An induction presentation will probably also involve the same house styles and copyright considerations as the newsletter task.

3. A spreadsheet solution to calculate pay is less likely to have house style and copyright issues, but will certainly have security and data protection implications (see next exercise).

Exercise 7 - Legal Constraints

Guidelines

IT and electronic communication now form an important part of many peoples' lives, so it is not surprising that a large amount of regulation and legislation exists to control it. Some of these could be constraints on how a solution is applied and some major examples are listed here.

- **Copyright**. Any image, text file or other item which may be copied from a site on the Internet is considered to be the copyright of the person or organisation that created it. So unless you have explicit permission, you cannot use or distribute any material obtained from the world wide web.

- **User Licence**. Normally when you buy any piece of software, you purchase a licence to use the software in a single location, so giving away copies for others to use is illegal. Organisations will often purchase multiple user licences. This allows them to run a certain number of copies (but no more) within their organisation.

- **Data Protection Act**. An organisation which stores any personal data referring to any identifiable individuals is bound by the current version of this Act. In summary, this requires that all such data shall be:

  o   Obtained and processed fairly and lawfully

  o   Processed only for one or more specified and lawful purposes

  o   Adequate, relevant and not excessive for those purposes

  o   Accurate and kept up to date

  o   Kept for the original purpose only and for no longer than is necessary.

  o   Processed in line with the rights of the individual

  o   Secure and protected against loss, damage and inappropriate processing

  o   Not transferred to countries unless they also have data protection

- **Computer Misuse Act**. This act covers the unauthorised access by individuals into computer systems, sometimes known as computer 'hacking'.

- **Consumer Rights**. In principle, buying goods or services electronically online is covered by the same consumer rights as buying from a shop, with some extra entitlements such as an order confirmation and a 'cooling off' period.

Exercise 7 - Continued

- **Health and Safety**. The Health and Safety at Work legislation (HASAW) has many regulations referring to computer installations regarding such issues as suitability and accessibility of equipment (keyboards, screens, mouse mats, etc.), and time spent using equipment.

- **Accessibility**. Computer installations should, wherever possible, be inaccessible to anyone regardless of their age, gender, origin or physical disability.

- **Inappropriate Content**. The displayed content of any computer system is governed by the same laws relating to offensive or obscene content as for printed material. In addition, individual organisations may have their own guidelines on this subject.

Examples

1. Copyright laws and regulations on inappropriate content would apply to the newsletter solution. If the solution involved installing new computers or software applications, then Health and Safety and User Licence rules may be relevant.

2. The presentation example will have the same considerations as the newsletter.

3. As the spreadsheet pay system will hold details referring to individuals, the security and legal constraints are likely to be much more significant.

    Access to the system should be limited to specific individuals (or departments), data files should be protected, and the person responsible for data protection should be made aware of the information that is being held within the system.

Exercise 8 - Revision

You are given a task to produce a mail shot which will be posted out as soon as possible to a large number of companies. All necessary details of these companies are available on a database file. Some selection of companies from the database will be involved, e.g. only companies from a specific area or town. The task is to be completed in a *Microsoft Office* environment. You decide to use the **mail merge** feature of *Microsoft Word* for the task.

1. Which of the following skills will be <u>necessary</u> for you to complete this task?

    a) Word processing skills

    b) Database skills

    c) Internet skills

    d) SQL skills

2. In the scenario above, which of the following resources will be <u>necessary</u> for you to complete this task?

    a) CD drive

    b) Printer

    c) Copy of *Microsoft Word*

    d) Copy of *Microsoft Access*

3. In the scenario above, the following are all reasons for choosing an IT solution based on *Word*. Which do you think is the most important in <u>this particular</u> example?

    a) Consistent quality of letter

    b) Will not require any extra staff resource

    c) Can be completed quickly

4. If you were asked to create a solution to maintain the sickness records of all members of staff in an organisation, which would be the main legal consideration?

    a) Health and Safety

    b) Data Protection

    c) Consumer rights

[i] *Check the answers at the back of the guide.*

Section 2
Create Solution

By the end of this Section you should be able to:

Use IT systems and software to complete planned tasks
and produce effective outcomes

Use shortcut techniques to improve overall efficiency

     © CiA Training Ltd 2009

Exercise 9 - Create a Solution

Guidelines

When all planning is complete, the actual solution can be created using the selected application. Whilst developing the solutions, always remain aware of the relevant points of the scenario specification and of the constraints and factors that may arise from them. Make sure the solution takes them all into account.

It is not the purpose of this unit to test knowledge of the individual applications. The technical level required should be no more than that covered by the appropriate specific units at this level, e.g. word processing, spreadsheets. To quote from the Assessment Specification for this unit, "Any aspect [required by the solution] that is unfamiliar will require support and advice from other people".

There are, however, some techniques specifically mentioned in the Assessment Specification for this unit that users may not have covered. The principles of these techniques will be described in the next exercises in this section.

Examples

1. Any solution may be expected to involve basic IT techniques such as:
    - Manipulation of files and folders
    - Data entry and editing
    - Transferring data between applications
    - Presenting all output to a professional standard

2. Producing a newsletter using *Word* could involve the following skills:
    - Formatting (fonts and backgrounds)
    - Column layout
    - Inserting text from other files (copy and paste will be adequate)
    - Inserting and manipulating images
    - Using visual effects such as *Clip Art* or *WordArt*.

3. The picture on the next page shows an example page of a suitable newsletter.

Exercise 9 - Continued

Newsletter

Friday 27th March 2009

New Contract

Yesterday saw the signing of a historic contract between Rutland Council and Barnacle Training to provide all training resources across the whole of the County.

Barnacle's chairman, Bill Barnacle said today that this represented a landmark achievement in the history of the company. "It will guarantee our future for years to come", he said. "Special praise is due to the sales team, headed by Lindsay Lafitte".

A program of recruitment for all job types is expected to start almost immediately to cope with the extra work generated by the contract.

Bounty

In view of the forthcoming recruitment campaign, any employee who successfully introduces a new starter to the company will earn a bounty payment of £200. This will be payable after the first 6 months of employment.

Wedding of the Year

June of this year will see the wedding of Sue Nightingale (Personnel) to Rocky Brown (Production). This is seen as a significant event, uniting as it does these two historic departments. The reception will be held in the canteen and senior management will be making an appearance.

Chef

This week we welcome back our famous chef Jim Tripe from his lengthy spell in hospital. Although the canteen has been ably managed in his absence, it will be good to get him back in charge and see the food return to its unique blend of quality and adventure.

Oldest Employee

Bob Ludd, 84, is retiring next week after 40 fine years of continuous service. Personnel Manager Brian Walders said "He should have gone years ago but we all forgot he was there".

Barnacle Training

Exercise 9 - Continued

4.   Producing an induction presentation using *PowerPoint* could involve the following skills:

   o   Slide formatting (fonts and backgrounds)

   o   Inserting text from other files (copy and paste will be adequate)

   o   Inserting and manipulating images

   o   Using visual effects such as *Clip Art* or *WordArt*

   o   Using simple animation effects

5.   The picture below shows four sample slides from a suitable presentation as an example

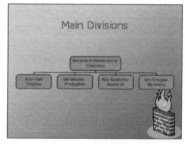

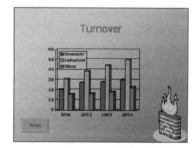

Exercise 9 - Continued

6. Producing an hourly pay spreadsheet using *Excel* could involve the following skills:

    o   Worksheet formatting (fonts and backgrounds)

    o   Inserting data from other files (copy and paste will be adequate)

    o   Wide range of formula

    o   Fixed referencing

    o   Totalling

7. The picture below shows a sample spreadsheet that could have been created as a solution.

Hourly Paid Employees
week commencing 30/03/2009   Basic Hours
                                                        40

No	Surname	First	Department	Rate	Total Hours	Bonuses	Gross Pay
1	Parke	Neil	Finishing	£12.00	30		£360.00
2	Patel	Ravinder	Finishing	£14.50	25		£362.50
3	Chesterton	Ian	Production	£10.00	50	50	£550.00
4	Smith	David	Testing	£14.00	40		£560.00
5	Waldram	Zara	Testing	£12.00	40		£480.00
6	Smith	James	Production	£10.00	40	50	£400.00
7	Waterman	David	Testing	£13.00	30		£390.00
8	Smith	John	Production	£10.00	40	50	£400.00
9	Westgarth	Shaun	Maintenance	£12.50	45		£593.75
10	McMillan	Rose	Production	£10.00	40	50	£400.00
11	Wright	Margaret	Production	£10.00	40	50	£400.00
12	Zapora	Androv	Maintenance	£12.50	45		£593.75
17	Singh	Vikram	Finishing	£11.00	40		£440.00
18	Oman	Tariq	Maintenance	£12.50	45		£593.75
19	Leigh	Clare	Maintenance	£12.50	30		£375.00
20	Chapman	Ian	Testing	£10.00	40		£400.00
21	Ripley	Ellen	Testing	£13.50	35		£472.50
22	Odara	Desmond	Production	£10.00	40	50	£400.00
23	Sovich	Mikhael	Production	£10.00	42	50	£430.00
							£8,601.25

Exercise 10 - Templates

Guidelines

A template is a blank framework of a document (or a spreadsheet or a presentation) which can be saved and used as the basic for future documents, etc. This can increase efficiency as the same layout does not have to be entered every time a new document is produced.

As an example, this exercise will demonstrate the creation of a template document in *Microsoft Word XP* or *2003*. Any difference in *2007* will be noted. The same principles apply to other applications.

It is assumed that the user is competent in the use of the relevant application, *Word* in this example. If not, read the exercise for information only, or consult a guide specific to the application.

Actions

1.   Start *Word* and create a new blank document.

2.   Type the title **Barnacle Training**. Change the font to **Tahoma** (or any other font), size **28pt**, and align the text centrally.

3.   Apply pale blue shading to the title text.

4.   Apply a **Page Border** of **1pt Shadow**.

5.   When all required formatting is applied, the document can be saved as a template. Select the **Save As** option.

6.   Enter a **File name** of **Barnacle** and in **Save as type**, select **Document Template**.

*Note: In Word 2007 the file extension is .**dotx**. Depending on the settings on your computer the file extension may not be shown at all.*

| File name: | Barnacle.dot |
| Save as type: | Document Template (*.dot) |

7.   Make sure the location for the save (**Save In**) is set to **Templates**. This may be set automatically or you may have to select it.

8.   Click **Save**. The template is saved for future use.

9.   **Close** the current document.

Exercise 11 - Macros

Guidelines

A **macro** records keystrokes and menu selections, then plays them back exactly as they were recorded. A macro can be created so that a commonly used task can be performed, or a word, phrase or paragraph can be entered automatically. The use of macros results in the more efficient production of documents. Once macros have been created, they can be used at any time in any document that uses the same template.

As an example, this exercise will demonstrate the creation of a macro in *Microsoft Word XP*. The same principles apply to other applications.

It is assumed that the user is competent in the use of the relevant application, *Word* in this example. If not, read the exercise for information only, or consult a guide specific to the application.

Actions

1. Create a new document in *Word.* Instead of creating a blank document, select **General Templates** from the **New Document** area (**My templates** in 2007).

2. Select the **Barnacle** template created in the previous exercise and click **OK**. A new document is created with all the content and formatting of the template.

3. Create three blank lines under the title and insert any picture or clip art from your computer. Make sure the image is selected.

4. Select **Tools | Macro | Record New Macro** (**Record Macro** button on the **Developer** tab in *2007*). Enter **Border** as the **Macro name**.

Exercise 11 - Continued

5.   Click **OK** to start recording the macro.

6.   Select **Format | Borders and Shading**.

*Note: In 2007, select **Borders and Shading** from the **Border** button in the **Paragraph** group on the **Home** tab.*

7.   Define a **3pt**, **Double Line** border in dark green and click **OK** to apply it to the image.

8.   Stop recording the macro.

9.   Add two more blank lines then insert another image.

10.   Select the image and select **Tools | Macro | Macros**.

*Note: In 2007 click the **Macros** button on the **Developer** tab.*

11.   Select the **Border** macro and click **Run**. The macro runs, applying the green border to the new picture.

12.   Save the document in **My Documents** (**Documents** in 2007) as **Barnacle2** and leave it open for the next exercise.

Exercise 12 - Shortcuts

Guidelines

There are various shortcuts that can be applied to IT solutions to make them more efficient. For example your toolbars can be customised to include shortcuts to any macros that have been created and shortcuts to files or applications can be included on your **Desktop**.

Actions

2007 users go to step **9**.

1. Users of *XP / 2003* select **Tools | Customize**.

2. Click on the **Commands** tab and scroll down the list of **Categories** until **Macros** appears.

3. Click on **Macros** to view all the macros created.

4. Click and drag **Normal.NewMacros.Border** up on to any toolbar. When the mouse is released a new button appears.

5. Click on **Modify Selection** in the **Customize** dialog box and in the **Name:** box, enter **Picture Border**.

6. Click on **Change Button Image**.

7. Select the **smiley face** from the choice of button icons.

8. Click **Close** to close the dialog box.

XP / 2003 users go to step **14**.

9. Users of *2007* right click on the **Quick Access Toolbar** and select **Customize Quick Access Toolbar**.

10. Click on the **Popular Commands** drop down arrow and select **Macros**.

11. Select the **Border** macro and click the **Add>>** button.

12. Click on **Modify**. Select the **smiley face** icon and in the **Display name:** box, enter **Picture Border**. Click **OK**.

13. Click **OK** to close the dialog box.

14. Insert another image into the document.

Exercise 12 - Continued

15. With the image selected, click the new button on the toolbar to run the macro. The green border will be applied.

16. To remove the new button from the toolbar, hold down the <**Alt**> key and drag the button down off the toolbar.

*Note: In 2007 right click the new button and select **Remove from Quick Access Toolbar**.*

17. Select **Tools | Macro | Macros**.

*Note: In 2007 click the **Macros** button on the **Developer** tab.*

18. To delete the macro, select the **Border** macro, then click **Delete**.

19. Select **Yes** at the prompt and click **Close**.

20. Close the document without saving and close *Word*.

21. Shortcuts can be made to files, folders or programs. Select **My Documents** (**Documents** in *2007*) from the **Start** menu.

22. Right click on the **Barnacle2** file and select **Send To**, then **Desktop (create shortcut)**.

23. Close the **My Documents** window (**Documents** in *2007*) and display your **Desktop**. There will be a shortcut icon on the **Desktop** for the file.

24. Double click on the icon. The **Barnacle2**document will be opened in *Word*.

25. Close the **Barnacle2**document and close *Word*.

26. To remove the icon from your **Desktop**, right click on it and select **Delete**. Click **Yes** at the prompt.

Exercise 13 - Revision

1. In which two of the following examples would the use of a template be the most appropriate?

    a) A monthly report showing the number of books borrowed from each section of a library

    b) A presentation showing your holiday photographs

    c) A rejection letter to unsuccessful job applicants

    d) A letter to a friend

2. Which of the following processes could best be replaced by a macro?

    a) Format each real name in a document as **Bold**

    b) Resize each image in a document as 10cm by 6cm with a dark blue border

    c) Crop each image in a document to highlight the relevant parts

3. Why is it appropriate to place a macro on a toolbar?

    a) Because it looks good

    b) Because it will not work otherwise

    c) Because it is more convenient to run

       © *CiA Training Ltd 2009*

Section 3
Review and Adapt

By the end of this Section you should be able to:

Review ongoing use of IT tools and techniques

Describe whether selected IT tools were appropriate

Analyse the strengths and weaknesses of the solution

Describe ways to make further improvements

Review solutions

Exercise 14 - Review Techniques

Guidelines

When the solution has been completed, and even while it is being developed, there should be a review of the effectiveness of the choices made. Information should be collected from a study of how the solution is operating.

There are many factors which can be considered when deciding whether the choice of tools and techniques were appropriate:

- Time. Has the time taken to develop the solution been in line with the original plan? Would it have been quicker to use any alternative methods?

- Cost. Similarly, has the cost of the development been as expected?

- Convenience. Has the choice of IT tools for the task resulted in a more convenient process in the solution? Would it have been easier to use any alternative methods?

- Quality/accuracy. Do the chosen IT tools provide sufficient quality and accuracy in the solution?

- Versatility. Has the choice of IT tools for the task resulted in a versatile process in the solution? Could it be easily adapted to other, related tasks? Could the information in the solution be easily presented in a different format, to be transferred to another application? Does the solution offer a range of functions and facilities?

- Information access. Are there any issues in accessing the necessary information for the solution? For example, does it require a network connection and/or a security password, or does it involve downloading data from the Internet? Downloading large amounts of data from the Internet can be a problem, particularly if only a slow speed Internet connection is available.

If any of the above factors indicated that the solution was not as efficient as it should be, you should be prepared to modify the approach as necessary.

Examples

1. For all the solutions, information should be collected on how well the outcome matches the requirements and how easily the outcome was achieved. Pay particular attention to whether the tools and techniques turned out to be appropriate. For example, do you think using *Word* to produce the newsletter was the best choice of application? Could it have been done better or quicker using any other techniques?

Exercise 15 - Analyse

Guidelines

As part of the review of the IT solution it is useful to analyse the performance of the final system in terms of strengths and weaknesses.

Potential areas of strength could include:

- Clarity. Does the format and layout of the final work make the presented information clear and easy to follow?

- Accuracy. Is all information presented accurately?

- Reliability. Can the solution be relied on to behave in a consistent manner and produce consistent information?

- Structure. Is all information presented in a logical, structured manner?

- Quality. Is the style and quality of the final work of a professional standard and does it create a good impression on the intended audience?

- Convenience. Is the solution is easy to use?

- Robustness. The solution should not fail, even under a range of conditions, and any exceptional conditions should be handled logically.

Potential areas of weakness would obviously include the reverse aspect of the features above:

- Muddled, unclear information.

- Inaccuracies in the presented information.

- Inconsistent behaviour and information.

- Unstructured information makes it difficult to locate required points.

- The style and quality of the final work is of a poor standard and creates a bad impression on the intended audience.

- The solution is not easy to use.

- System prone to failing, locking, etc., with no adequate recovery procedures.

Exercise 15 - Continued

Examples

1. In the newsletter scenario, is the included information all relevant and presented in a clear and accurate way? Is there a template available and will it be relevant to future editions? Does the format make the information easy to read and understand?

2. In the presentation scenario all of the above are relevant. Also, do the transitions and other animations detract from the overall effectiveness?

3. In the spreadsheet scenario has all input data been checked for accuracy? Has it been entered correctly? Are all formulae checked and accurate? Will the format be practical for all forms of data? Is it easy to input data?

Exercise 16 - Review Outcomes

Guidelines

A detailed review of the actual output from the solution is an important feature of the task. The first reason for doing this is to check the solution with the aims and plans for the project to ensure that the original requirements have been met. The second reason is to correct any errors, omissions or unwanted side effects that may exist within the solution.

Steps that could be involved in this process include:

- Checking the solutions against the original requirements. This is where written evidence of the aims and objectives of the task would be very useful.

- Consulting with the intended audience/users of the solution to see if the solution meets their requirements and expectations.

- Producing sample outputs (drafts) from the system for analysis.

- Checking the quality of the source information.

- Spell check and proof read all output text. Note that spell checking will only identify unrecognised words. It will not generally find words used incorrectly, e.g. *horse* instead of *house*, or *her* instead of *here*, so manual proof reading is always recommended.

- If the solution depends on numerical calculations, make sure they are tested with dummy data and compare the results with the expected results obtained by manual calculation. Ideally the solution will be tested with a range of input data, including extreme values to check that they are handled correctly.

- Check all output for suitability so that it will not cause offence to any member of the target audience.

- Check all output for compliance with legal requirements such as copyright or data protection laws.

- Be aware of what effect any mistakes in your solution will have on others.

Exercise 16 - Continued

Examples

1. Check that the newsletter meets the original requirements. Is it eye catching and professional looking? Is it free from spelling and grammar mistakes? Make sure that it does not contain any offensive, inappropriate or copyright protected content.

2. Check that the presentation meets the original requirements. Is it a free running, looping presentation? Does it display relevant summary information in a professional way? Check with users that it communicates the desired information. Make sure that it does not contain any offensive, inappropriate or copyright protected content.

3. Check that the spreadsheet meets the original requirements. Is all starting data correctly set up? Does it allow data to be entered easily and produce accurate results? Are users of the system happy that they can operate it satisfactorily and that it supplies them with the information that they need?

Exercise 17 - Improvements

Guidelines

After testing and reviewing the solution, it may become clear that there are a variety of ways in which the work could be improved.

- Correcting any mistakes. This will obviously improve the quality of the work.

- Responding to feedback. It may become obvious when the solution is actually operating that there is a better way for parts of the process to work. For example, these may make the overall process easier to use or less prone to errors.

- Learning new techniques. This may mean that some features of the project could be achieved in different ways, which would improve the operation of the solution.

- Adding automated IT features to the solution such as macros and shortcuts. This will improve the efficiency of the solution.

- In systems that require input of data, the data entry interfaces could be streamlined to increase efficiency.

- Minimising the impact that the new system has on other peoples' work. The effectiveness of a solution is reduced if it requires an increase in work in a different area.

Examples

1. Any solution should be analysed with respect to the points listed above.

Exercise 18 - Revision

You are given a task to produce a mail shot which will be posted out as soon as possible to a large number of companies. All necessary details of these companies are available on a database file. Some selection of companies from the database will be involved, e.g. only companies from a specific area or town. The task is to be completed in a *Microsoft Office* environment.

1. Which two of these statements best confirms that the chosen IT solution was appropriate for the task?

    a) "We will be doing another mailshot next month."

    b) "We will need a better printer for these mailshots."

    c) "Well done, the mailshot went out on time and to the correct companies."

    d) "This was the most effective mailshot we have ever done."

2. From the following statements, pick one which represents a strength of the solution and one which represents a weakness.

    a) The printer is running out of toner

    b) The details in the database of companies is not kept up to date

    c) It is easy to select different companies from the database

    d) All the mailshot letters look the same

3. Which two of the following would best represent an improvement to your solution?

    a) Spell and grammar check the letter

    b) Change the password on the system

    c) Use a cheaper printer

    d) Print labels at the same time as the letters

Section 4
Develop and Test

By the end of this Section you should be able to:

Review the benefits and drawbacks of IT tools

Describe ways to increase productivity and efficiency

Develop solutions to improve own productivity

Test solutions to ensure they work as intended

Exercise 19 - Review Benefits

Guidelines

Using IT tools to develop solutions in a business environment will usually produce both benefits and drawbacks with respect to productivity. Some of these have been discussed in the course of this guide but they can be summarised here.

Benefits:

- Faster achievement of output

- Higher quality output

- More automated system – frees staff for other tasks

- Less need for outside specialists

- More consistent, reliable output

- Ability to integrate with other IT systems

Drawbacks:

- Cost of development

- Retraining costs

- Cost of extra resources, e.g. computers

- Dependence on technology

Examples

1. The main benefits of the newsletter solution are that it produces a high quality outcome quickly and without the need for specialist staff.

2. The main benefits of the presentation solution are that it produces a high quality outcome which is easily accessible, without the need for specialist staff.

3. The main benefits of the spreadsheet solution are that it produces a consistent, reliable outcome with a minimum of staff intervention and has the potential to streamline business operations by integrating with other processes.

Exercise 20 - Develop Solutions

Guidelines

When the IT solution is reviewed, it may become clear that changes could be made which would improve the productivity and efficiency. There are different ways to improve productivity and efficiency of a process:

- Achieve the same result in less time

- Achieve the same result for less money

- Achieve greater output in the same time

- Achieve higher quality output

- Free staff for other tasks

- Any improvement in productivity would have to be balanced against the cost of developing the solution

One way to make IT solutions more productive is to reduce the manual component of the task and allow the computer to handle more of it, i.e. to have more automated processes.

For example you could use conditional calculations to deal with different situations automatically without user intervention, e.g. calculate different discount rates depending on the total sales value for a record.

Any features where data may be picked up automatically rather than have to be manually processed will make the solution quicker and easier to operate, less likely to produce errors, and therefore more efficient.

When data from external sources is required within a system, it is usually better to create a link to that data rather than copy it or re-enter it. Linking to external data means that whenever the source data is changed in any way, the most recent version of that data will always be used without any user intervention.

Other examples of automated features would be:

- Use a macro, so that one action by the user can run a series of processes in a fixed sequence

- Create shortcuts so that commonly used features can be started quickly

- Customise menus and toolbars to include shortcuts and macros

- Create templates so that consistent results can be achieved more quickly if the task is required again

For anyone unfamiliar with any of the points above, section 2 of this guide includes some relevant technical exercises.

Exercise 20 - Continued

Examples

1. The productivity of the newsletter task could be improved by creating a template for the solution before any content is added. Subsequent releases of the newsletter could then be produced merely by opening the template and adding new content.

2. If the induction presentation is a one-off project that is running automatically, then there is not much scope for increasing productivity. Linking the slide content to *Word* documents would mean that updates could be made easily to the documents using *Word* and these changes would be automatically reflected in the presentation. Defining a template with master slides would benefit the production of any future versions of the presentation.

3. A template of the payroll spreadsheet would make it easy to produce new spreadsheets for each week. Data validation could reduce the possibility of input errors and conditional formatting could highlight exceptional results. If the output from this system could be used as input to the next stage of the payroll process, this would avoid unnecessary re-keying of data.

Exercise 21 - Test Solution

Guidelines

The final version of the developed solution should always be tested.

- As mentioned previously, it is important that the results of the task are compared to the original plan requirements.

- A final check can be made of spelling, calculations and content.

- Particularly check any automated features or improvements which have been added to the solution later in the process. Do any templates, macros and shortcuts work as intended?

Examples

1. Check that the newsletter meets the original requirements. Is it free from spelling and grammar mistakes? If there is a template for the finished solution, does it open and allow content to be easily added?

2. Check that the presentation meets the original requirements. If there are links to any external material, do the links work correctly? If there is a template for the finished solution, does it open and allow content to be easily added?

3. Check that the spreadsheet meets the original requirements. If there are any automated features, do they work as intended? If there are any added features such as data export of reports, do they work as intended?

Exercise 22 - Revision

1.   In terms of productivity, divide the following statements into those which represent a benefit of using an IT solution for a task and those which represent a drawback (compared with an alternative non-IT solution).

       a) The task does not require as many staff to operate it

       b) The task requires more people to operate it

       c) The task requires highly skilled people to operate it

       d) The task requires expensive computer equipment

       e) The task can be completed in less time

       f) The task requires only existing computer equipment

2.   Which two of the following would be ways of increasing the productivity of your completed task?

       a) Automate more of the functions within the solution

       b) Increase the number of different applications used in the solution

       c) Add shortcuts to save time when running the solution

       d) Add a musical background

Exercise 23 - Summary

Guidelines

The assessment for this unit will be in two parts.

The learner will be given a scenario requiring an IT solution and it will be necessary for them to create a solution which meets the requirements of the scenario. This will include selecting the appropriate software application for the task. Initially the choice of applications will only include word processing, presentations, or spreadsheets.

All required content, text, numbers, images will be provided.

Additionally there will be a multi choice question paper of 12 questions which cover some of the content of the unit.

Answers

Exercise 8

Step1   **a)** Only word processing skills are necessary. The required database processing can be done entirely within *Word*.

Step 2   **b)** and **c)** A *Word* application is required to create the mail shot and a printer will be require to print out the letters.

Step 3   **c)** One of the requirements was to produce the mail shot as quickly as possible.

Step 4   **b)** If you hold information about identifiable individuals, the Data Protection laws are of primary importance.

Exercise 13

Step 1   **a)** and **c)** These are more likely to have the same framework each time they are run.

Step 2   **b)** This is would replace a number of identical steps. A macro could be written for **a)** but it would be no easier than clicking the **Bold** button. The steps in **c)** are likely to be different every time.

Step 3   **c)**

Exercise 18

Step 1   **c)** and **d)** These refer to the choice of solution.

Step 2   **c)** would represent a strength, **b)** would represent a weakness.

Step 3   **a)** and **d)** Both of these would improve the solution.

Exercise 22

Step 1   Benefits **a)**, **e)**, **f)**.

              Drawbacks **b)**, **c)**, **d)**

Step 2   **a)** and **c)** would be the most likely to improve the productivity of the solution.

Glossary

Animation	In presentations, a motion effect which affects objects on a slide or the transition between slides.
Application	A software program such as *Word*.
Clip Art	A range of images available within *Microsoft Office* applications which can be inserted into documents, etc.
Commands	Selections from the **Menu Bar** which perform actions.
Download	Transfer an object from a web site to the user's computer.
Firewall	A filter to control traffic from your PC to the Internet and vice versa.
Font	A type or style of print.
Formatting	Change the way a document, etc. looks.
House Style	A standard set of layout and formatting rules that are applied to all documents, etc. within an organisation.
Linking	Creating a pointer to another item rather than including a copy of it.
Logo	Small, simple graphic that is used to represent an organisation.
Macro	Set of commands that can be run.
Mail Merge	Combining a main *Word* document with a data source.
Print Preview	A feature that shows how a document will look before it is printed.
Resources	Anything that is a requirement for task, such as people, equipment, software.
Ribbon	The equivalent of the toolbars in *Office 2007*.
Template	A framework or base document, etc. that contains certain elements and can be used over and over again to produce consistent output.
Virus	Malicious piece of program designed to enter your system unnoticed.
WordArt	A feature in *Microsoft Word* which allows text to be added as an image.

Index

Other Products from CiA Training

CiA Training Ltd is a leading publishing company, which has consistently delivered the highest quality products since 1985. A wide range of flexible and easy to use self teach resources has been developed by CiA's experienced publishing team to aid the learning process. These include the following related products at the time of publication of this product:

- **BCS IT Security Level 1**

- **ECDL/ICDL Syllabus 5.0**

- **ECDL/ICDL Advanced Syllabus 2.0**

- **ECDL/ICDL Revision Series**

- **ECDL/ICDL Advanced Syllabus 2.0 Revision Series**

Previous syllabus versions also available - contact us for further details.

We hope you have enjoyed using our materials and would love to hear your opinions about them. If you'd like to give us some feedback, please go to:

www.ciatraining.co.uk/feedback.php

and let us know what you think.

New products are constantly being developed. For up to the minute information on our products, to view our full range, to find out more, or to be added to our mailing list, visit:

www.ciatraining.co.uk

SOUTHAMPTON
CITY COLLEGE
LEARNING CENTRE